2022

Weekly & Monthly Planner

This Planner Belongs To:

Vision Board

RELATIONSHIPS

FUN & RECREATION

FAMILY

LOVE

HEALTH

SPIRITUALITY

SOCIAL

PERSONAL DEVELOPMENT

CAREER

KNOWLEDGE

SKILLS

FINANCE

Bucket List

TRY

VISIT &
EXPLORE

CREATE

PLAY

LEARN &
READ

COOK &
EAT

MAKE

WATCH

2022

January

S	M	T	W	T	F	S
						1
2	3	4	5	6	7	8
9	10	11	12	13	14	15
16	17	18	19	20	21	22
23	24	25	26	27	28	29
30	31					

February

S	M	T	W	T	F	S
		1	2	3	4	5
6	7	8	9	10	11	12
13	14	15	16	17	18	19
20	21	22	23	24	25	26
27	28					

March

S	M	T	W	T	F	S
		1	2	3	4	5
6	7	8	9	10	11	12
13	14	15	16	17	18	19
20	21	22	23	24	25	26
27	28	29	30	31		

April

S	M	T	W	T	F	S
					1	2
3	4	5	6	7	8	9
10	11	12	13	14	15	16
17	18	19	20	21	22	23
24	25	26	27	28	29	30

May

S	M	T	W	T	F	S
1	2	3	4	5	6	7
8	9	10	11	12	13	14
15	16	17	18	19	20	21
22	23	24	25	26	27	28
29	30	31				

June

S	M	T	W	T	F	S
			1	2	3	4
5	6	7	8	9	10	11
12	13	14	15	16	17	18
19	20	21	22	23	24	25
26	27	28	29	30		

July

S	M	T	W	T	F	S
					1	2
3	4	5	6	7	8	9
10	11	12	13	14	15	16
17	18	19	20	21	22	23
24	25	26	27	28	29	30
31						

August

S	M	T	W	T	F	S
	1	2	3	4	5	6
7	8	9	10	11	12	13
14	15	16	17	18	19	20
21	22	23	24	25	26	27
28	29	30	31			

September

S	M	T	W	T	F	S
				1	2	3
4	5	6	7	8	9	10
11	12	13	14	15	16	17
18	19	20	21	22	23	24
25	26	27	28	29	30	

October

S	M	T	W	T	F	S
						1
2	3	4	5	6	7	8
9	10	11	12	13	14	15
16	17	18	19	20	21	22
23	24	25	26	27	28	29
30	31					

November

S	M	T	W	T	F	S
		1	2	3	4	5
6	7	8	9	10	11	12
13	14	15	16	17	18	19
20	21	22	23	24	25	26
27	28	29	30			

December

S	M	T	W	T	F	S
				1	2	3
4	5	6	7	8	9	10
11	12	13	14	15	16	17
18	19	20	21	22	23	24
25	26	27	28	29	30	31

Holidays

Name	2022	2023	2024
New Year's Day	Jan-01	Jan-01	Jan-01
Martin Luther King Jr. Day	Jan-17	Jan-16	Jan-14
Chinese New Year	Feb-01	Jan-22	Jan-10
Super Bowl	Feb-06	Feb-05	Feb-11
Valentine's Day	Feb-14	Feb-14	Feb-14
Presidents' Day	Feb-21	Feb-20	Feb-19
Ash Wednesday	Mar-02	Feb-22	Feb-14
Daylight Saving Time Begins	Mar-13	Mar-12	Mar-10
St. Patrick's Day	Mar-17	Mar-17	Mar-17
First Day of Spring	Mar-20	Mar-20	Mar-19
Palm Sunday	Apr-10	Apr-02	Mar-24
Passover, Begins at Sunset	Apr-15	Apr-05	Apr-22
Good Friday	Apr-15	Apr-07	Mar-29
Easter Sunday	Apr-17	Apr-09	Mar-31
Easter Monday	Apr-18	Apr-10	Apr-01
Earth Day	Apr-22	Apr-22	Apr-22
Cinco de Mayo	May-05	May-05	May-05
Mother's Day	May-08	May-14	May-12
Memorial Day	May-30	May-29	May-27
Father's Day	Jun-19	Jun-18	Jun-16
First Day of Summer	Jun-21	Jun-21	Jun-20
Independence Day	Jul-04	Jul-04	Jul-04
Labor Day	Sep-05	Sep-04	Sep-02
Patriot Day	Sep-11	Sep-11	Sep-11
National Grandparents Day	Sep-11	Sep-10	Sep-08
First Day of Autumn	Sep-22	Sep-23	Sep-22
Rosh Hashanah, Begins at Sunset	Sep-25	Sep-15	Oct-02
Yom Kippur, Begins at Sunset	Oct-04	Sep-24	Oct-11
Columbus Day	Oct-10	Oct-09	Oct-14
Halloween	Oct-31	Oct-31	Oct-31
Daylight Saving Time Ends	Nov-06	Nov-05	Nov-03
Election Day	Nov-08	Nov-07	Nov-05
Veterans Day	Nov-11	Nov-11	Nov-11
Thanksgiving Day	Nov-24	Nov-23	Nov-28
Black Friday	Nov-25	Nov-24	Nov-29
Cyber Monday	Nov-28	Nov-27	Dec-02
Hanukkah, Begins at Sunset	Dec-18	Dec-07	Dec-25
First Day of Winter	Dec-21	Dec-21	Dec-21
Christmas Eve	Dec-24	Dec-24	Dec-24
Christmas Day	Dec-25	Dec-25	Dec-25
New Year's Eve	Dec-31	Dec-31	Dec-31

Contacts

Name:

Address:

Phone:

Email:

Name:

Address:

Phone:

Email:

Name:

Address:

Phone:

Email:

Name:

Address:

Phone:

Email:

Name:

Address:

Phone:

Email:

Name:

Address:

Phone:

Email:

Name:

Address:

Phone:

Email:

Name:

Address:

Phone:

Email:

Name:

Address:

Phone:

Email:

Name:

Address:

Phone:

Email:

Name:

Address:

Phone:

Email:

Name:

Address:

Phone:

Email:

Contacts

Name:	Name:
Address:	Address:
Phone:	Phone:
Email:	Email:

Name:	Name:
Address:	Address:
Phone:	Phone:
Email:	Email:

Name:	Name:
Address:	Address:
Phone:	Phone:
Email:	Email:

Name:	Name:
Address:	Address:
Phone:	Phone:
Email:	Email:

Name:	Name:
Address:	Address:
Phone:	Phone:
Email:	Email:

Name:	Name:
Address:	Address:
Phone:	Phone:
Email:	Email:

Birthdays

JANUARY

- ⬡ _____
- ⬡ _____
- ⬡ _____
- ⬡ _____
- ⬡ _____
- ⬡ _____
- ⬡ _____
- ⬡ _____

FEBRUARY

- ⬡ _____
- ⬡ _____
- ⬡ _____
- ⬡ _____
- ⬡ _____
- ⬡ _____
- ⬡ _____
- ⬡ _____

MARCH

- ⬡ _____
- ⬡ _____
- ⬡ _____
- ⬡ _____
- ⬡ _____
- ⬡ _____
- ⬡ _____
- ⬡ _____

APRIL

- ⬡ _____
- ⬡ _____
- ⬡ _____
- ⬡ _____
- ⬡ _____
- ⬡ _____
- ⬡ _____
- ⬡ _____

MAY

- ⬡ _____
- ⬡ _____
- ⬡ _____
- ⬡ _____
- ⬡ _____
- ⬡ _____
- ⬡ _____
- ⬡ _____

JUNE

- ⬡ _____
- ⬡ _____
- ⬡ _____
- ⬡ _____
- ⬡ _____
- ⬡ _____
- ⬡ _____
- ⬡ _____

Birthdays

JULY

- ⬡ _____
- ⬡ _____
- ⬡ _____
- ⬡ _____
- ⬡ _____
- ⬡ _____
- ⬡ _____
- ⬡ _____

AUGUST

- ⬡ _____
- ⬡ _____
- ⬡ _____
- ⬡ _____
- ⬡ _____
- ⬡ _____
- ⬡ _____
- ⬡ _____

SEPTEMBER

- ⬡ _____
- ⬡ _____
- ⬡ _____
- ⬡ _____
- ⬡ _____
- ⬡ _____
- ⬡ _____
- ⬡ _____

OCTOBER

- ⬡ _____
- ⬡ _____
- ⬡ _____
- ⬡ _____
- ⬡ _____
- ⬡ _____
- ⬡ _____
- ⬡ _____

NOVEMBER

- ⬡ _____
- ⬡ _____
- ⬡ _____
- ⬡ _____
- ⬡ _____
- ⬡ _____
- ⬡ _____
- ⬡ _____

DECEMBER

- ⬡ _____
- ⬡ _____
- ⬡ _____
- ⬡ _____
- ⬡ _____
- ⬡ _____
- ⬡ _____
- ⬡ _____

01

Notes

January

Sunday	Monday	Tuesday
26	27	28
2	3	4
9	10	11
16	Martin luther king jr. Day 17	18
23	24	25
30	31	1

2022

Wednesday	Thursday	Friday	Saturday
			NEW YEAR'S DAY
29	30	31	1
5	6	7	8
12	13	14	15
19	20	21	22
26	27	28	29
2	3	4	5

January

S	M	T	W	T	F	S
						1
2	3	4	5	6	7	8
9	10	11	12	13	14	15
16	17	18	19	20	21	22
23	24	25	26	27	28	29
30	31					

Priorities

No. 1

No. 2

No. 3

Goals

1.

2.

3.

4.

5.

Activities & Fitness

Mon

Tue

Wed

Thur

Fri

Sat

Sun

"Success doesn't come from what you do occasionally, it comes from what you do consistently."

27
Monday

28
Tuesday

29
Wednesday

30
Thursday

31
Friday

1
Saturday

Notes

2
Sunday

January

S	M	T	W	T	F	S
						1
2	3	4	5	6	7	8
9	10	11	12	13	14	15
16	17	18	19	20	21	22
23	24	25	26	27	28	29
30	31					

Priorities

No. 1 ....

No. 2 ....

No. 3 ....

Goals

1. ....
2. ....
3. ....
4. ....
5. ....

Activities & Fitness

Mon ....

Tue ....

Wed ....

Thur ....

Fri ....

Sat ....

Sun ....

*"Doubt kills more dreams
than failure will ever."*

3
Monday

4
Tuesday

5
Wednesday

6
Thursday

This week
I am grateful for

Notes

7
Friday

8
Saturday

9
Sunday

January

S	M	T	W	T	F	S
						1
2	3	4	5	6	7	8
9	10	11	12	13	14	15
16	17	18	19	20	21	22
23	24	25	26	27	28	29
30	31					

Priorities

No. 1 ....

No. 2 ....

No. 3 ....

Goals

1. ....
2. ....
3. ....
4. ....
5. ....

Activities & Fitness

Mon ....

Tue ....

Wed ....

Thur ....

Fri ....

Sat ....

Sun ....

"Take massive, imperfect action towards your goals. The time will never be just right."

10
Monday

11
Tuesday

12
Wednesday

13
Thursday

Notes

14
Friday

15
Saturday

16
Sunday

January

S	M	T	W	T	F	S
						1
2	3	4	5	6	7	8
9	10	11	12	13	14	15
16	17	18	19	20	21	22
23	24	25	26	27	28	29
30	31					

Priorities

No. 1

No. 2

No. 3

Goals

1.

2.

3.

4.

5.

Activities & Fitness

Mon

Tue

Wed

Thur

Fri

Sat

Sun

"Be the girl who decided to go for it."

17
Monday

18
Tuesday

19
Wednesday

20
Thursday

Notes

21
Friday

22
Saturday

23
Sunday

January

S	M	T	W	T	F	S
						1
2	3	4	5	6	7	8
9	10	11	12	13	14	15
16	17	18	19	20	21	22
23	24	25	26	27	28	29
30	31					

Priorities

No. 1

No. 2

No. 3

Goals

1.

2.

3.

4.

5.

Activities & Fitness

Mon

Tue

Wed

Thur

Fri

Sat

Sun

"Thoughts have energy; make sure yours are positive."

24
Monday

25
Tuesday

26
Wednesday

27
Thursday

Notes

28
Friday

29
Saturday

30
Sunday

Habit Tracker

COLOR   ESSENTIAL HABITS

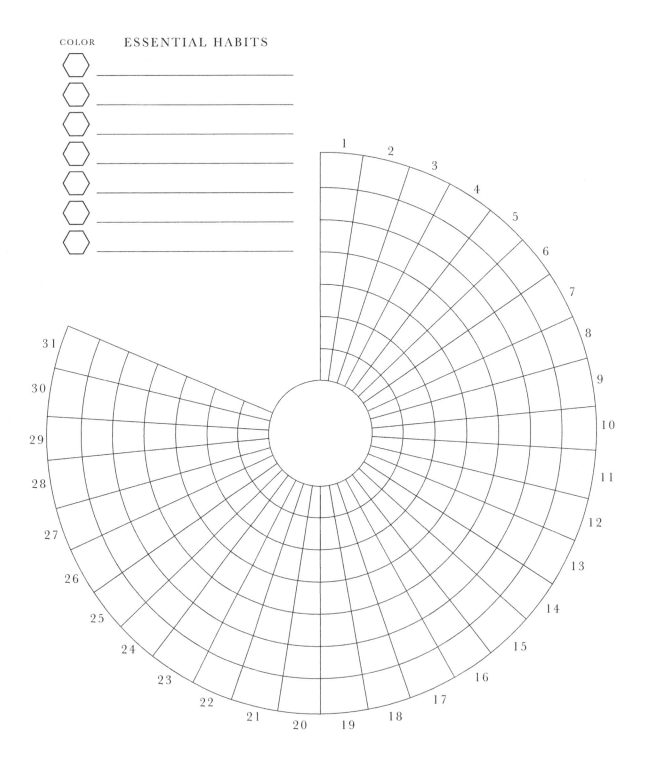

Mood Tracker

COLOR YOUR MOOD

HAPPY	SAD	TIRED	MOTIVATED	SICK
☐	☐	☐	☐	☐

FOCUSED	STRESSED	EXCITED	ANGRY	ANXIOUS
☐	☐	☐	☐	☐

02

February

Sunday	Monday	Tuesday
30	31	CHINESE NEW YEAR 1
SUPER BOWL 6	7	8
13	VALENTINE'S DAY 14	15
20	PRESIDENTS' DAY 21	22
27	28	1

*"Nothing is impossible, the word itself
says 'I'm possible'!"*
- AUDREY HEPBURN

2022

Wednesday	Thursday	Friday	Saturday
2	3	4	5
9	10	11	12
16	17	18	19
23	24	25	26
2	3	4	5

February

S	M	T	W	T	F	S
		1	2	3	4	5
6	7	8	9	10	11	12
13	14	15	16	17	18	19
20	21	22	23	24	25	26
27	28					

Priorities

No. 1 ....

No. 2 ....

No. 3 ....

Goals

1. ....

2. ....

3. ....

4. ....

5. ....

Activities & Fitness

Mon ....

Tue ....

Wed ....

Thur ....

Fri ....

Sat ....

Sun ....

*"He asked, What's your favorite position;
I said, CEO."*

31
Monday

1
Tuesday

2
Wednesday

3
Thursday

Notes

4
Friday

5
Saturday

6
Sunday

February

S	M	T	W	T	F	S
			1	2	3	4	5
6	7	8	9	10	11	12
13	14	15	16	17	18	19
20	21	22	23	24	25	26
27	28					

Priorities

No. 1

No. 2

No. 3

Goals

1.

2.

3.

4.

5.

Activities & Fitness

Mon

Tue

Wed

Thur

Fri

Sat

Sun

"Old ways won't open new doors."

7
Monday

8
Tuesday

9
Wednesday

10
Thursday

Notes

11
Friday

12
Saturday

13
Sunday

February

S	M	T	W	T	F	S
		1	2	3	4	5
6	7	8	9	10	11	12
13	14	15	16	17	18	19
20	21	22	23	24	25	26
27	28					

Priorities

No. 1

No. 2

No. 3

Goals

1.

2.

3.

4.

5.

Activities & Fitness

Mon

Tue

Wed

Thur

Fri

Sat

Sun

"Build a life you don't need a vacation from."

14
Monday

15
Tuesday

16
Wednesday

17
Thursday

18
Friday

19
Saturday

Notes

20
Sunday

February

S	M	T	W	T	F	S
		1	2	3	4	5
6	7	8	9	10	11	12
13	14	15	16	17	18	19
20	21	22	23	24	25	26
27	28					

Priorities

No. 1

No. 2

No. 3

Goals

1.

2.

3.

4.

5.

Activities & Fitness

Mon

Tue

Wed

Thur

Fri

Sat

Sun

"Your self worth is not determined by other's opinions."

21
Monday

22
Tuesday

23
Wednesday

24
Thursday

Notes

25
Friday

26
Saturday

27
Sunday

Habit Tracker

COLOR   ESSENTIAL HABITS

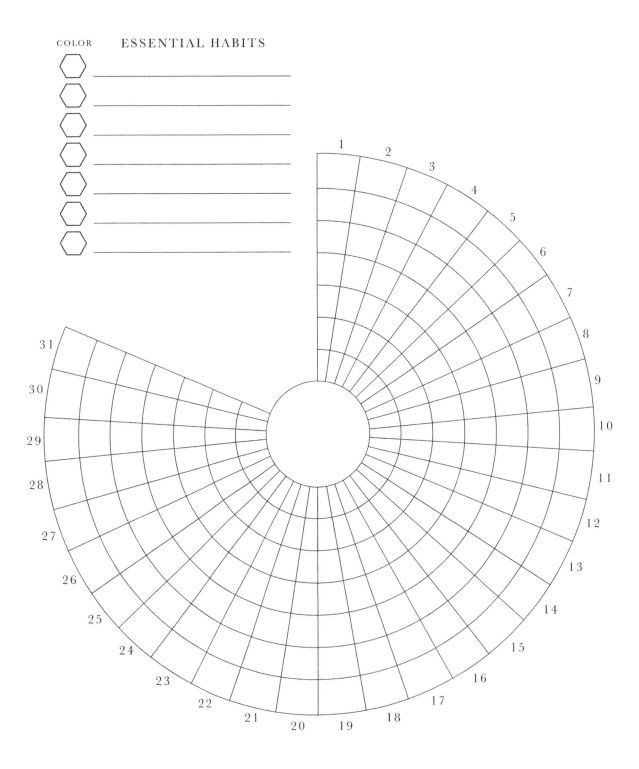

Mood Tracker

COLOR YOUR MOOD

HAPPY	SAD	TIRED	MOTIVATED	SICK

FOCUSED	STRESSED	EXCITED	ANGRY	ANXIOUS

03

March

Sunday	Monday	Tuesday
27	28	1
6	7	8
DAYLIGHT SAVING TIME BEGINS 13	14	15
FIRST DAY OF SPRING 20	21	22
27	28	29

Wednesday	Thursday	Friday	Saturday
ASH WEDNESDAY 2	 3	 4	 5
  9	 10	 11	 12
  16	ST. PATRICK'S DAY 17	 18	 19
  23	 24	 25	 26
  30	 31	 1	 2

March

S	M	T	W	T	F	S
		1	2	3	4	5
6	7	8	9	10	11	12
13	14	15	16	17	18	19
20	21	22	23	24	25	26
27	28	29	30	31		

Priorities

No. 1 ....

No. 2 ....

No. 3 ....

Goals

1. ....
2. ....
3. ....
4. ....
5. ....

Activities & Fitness

Mon ....

Tue ....

Wed ....

Thur ....

Fri ....

Sat ....

Sun ....

"The key to success is to start before you're ready."

28
Monday

1
Tuesday

2
Wednesday

3
Thursday

4
Friday

5
Saturday

*This week
I am grateful for*

Notes

6
Sunday

March

S	M	T	W	T	F	S
		1	2	3	4	5
6	7	8	9	10	11	12
13	14	15	16	17	18	19
20	21	22	23	24	25	26
27	28	29	30	31		

Priorities

No. 1 ....

No. 2 ....

No. 3 ....

Goals

1. ....

2. ....

3. ....

4. ....

5. ....

Activities & Fitness

Mon ....

Tue ....

Wed ....

Thur ....

Fri ....

Sat ....

Sun ....

"One day? Or Day One. You decide."

7
Monday

8
Tuesday

9
Wednesday

10
Thursday

11
Friday

12
Saturday

Notes

13
Sunday

March

S	M	T	W	T	F	S
		1	2	3	4	5
6	7	8	9	10	11	12
13	14	15	16	17	18	19
20	21	22	23	24	25	26
27	28	29	30	31		

Priorities

No. 1 ....

No. 2 ....

No. 3 ....

Goals

1. ....
2. ....
3. ....
4. ....
5. ....

Activities & Fitness

Mon ....

Tue ....

Wed ....

Thur ....

Fri ....

Sat ....

Sun ....

"Set goals that makes you want to JUMP out of bed in the morning!."

14
Monday

15
Tuesday

16
Wednesday

17
Thursday

18
Friday

18
Saturday

*This week
I am grateful for*

Notes

20
Sunday

March

S	M	T	W	T	F	S
		1	2	3	4	5
6	7	8	9	10	11	12
13	14	15	16	17	18	19
20	21	22	23	24	25	26
27	28	29	30	31		

Priorities

No. 1 ....

No. 2 ....

No. 3 ....

Goals

1. ....
2. ....
3. ....
4. ....
5. ....

Activities & Fitness

Mon ....

Tue ....

Wed ....

Thur ....

Fri ....

Sat ....

Sun ....

"Look at every setback as a sign from the universe on how to move forward in a new & better way."

21
Monday

22
Tuesday

23
Wednesday

24
Thursday

Notes

25
Friday

26
Saturday

27
Sunday

Habit Tracker

COLOR   ESSENTIAL HABITS

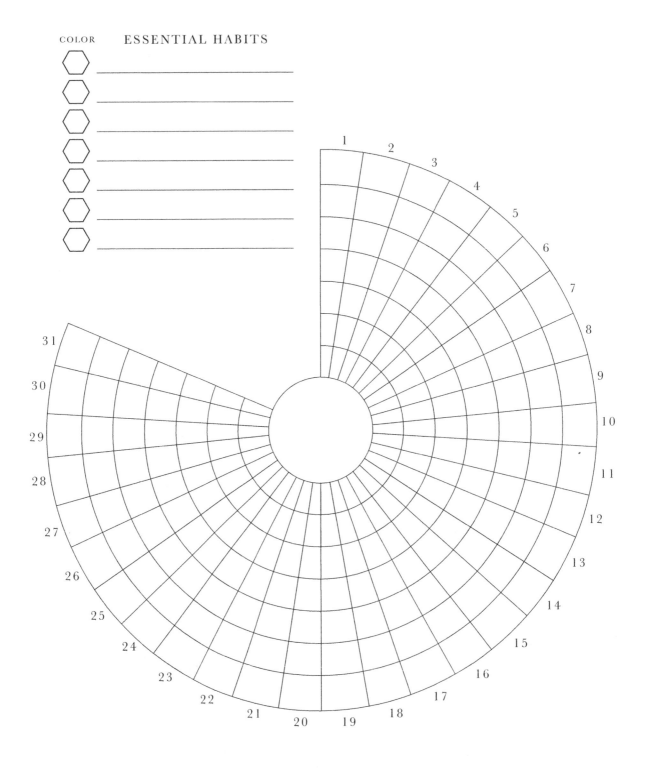

Mood Tracker

COLOR YOUR MOOD

HAPPY	SAD	TIRED	MOTIVATED	SICK
☐	☐	☐	☐	☐

FOCUSED	STRESSED	EXCITED	ANGRY	ANXIOUS
☐	☐	☐	☐	☐

1 8 2 7 17
12 6 25
24 14 4
23 20 31
30 10
29 5 19
21 27 15
18 11
3 26 13
16 9
28 22

04

April

Sunday	Monday	Tuesday
27	28	29
3	4	5
PALM SUNDAY 10	11	12
EASTER SUNDAY 17	EASTER MONDAY 18	19
24	25	26

2022

Wednesday	Thursday	Friday	Saturday
30	31	1	2
6	7	8	9
13	14	Passover, Begins at Sunset Good Friday 15	16
20	21	Earth Day 22	23
27	28	29	30

April

S	M	T	W	T	F	S
					1	2
3	4	5	6	7	8	9
10	11	12	13	14	15	16
17	18	19	20	21	22	23
24	25	26	27	28	29	30

Priorities

No. 1

No. 2

No. 3

Goals

1.

2.

3.

4.

5.

Activities & Fitness

Mon

Tue

Wed

Thur

Fri

Sat

Sun

"Be the woman you want your daughter to be."

28
Monday

29
Tuesday

30
Wednesday

31
Thursday

1
Friday

2
Saturday

Notes

3
Sunday

April

S	M	T	W	T	F	S
					1	2
3	4	5	6	7	8	9
10	11	12	13	14	15	16
17	18	19	20	21	22	23
24	25	26	27	28	29	30

Priorities

No. 1

No. 2

No. 3

Goals

1.

2.

3.

4.

5.

Activities & Fitness

Mon

Tue

Wed

Thur

Fri

Sat

Sun

"Strong women don't have attitudes, they have standards. "

4
Monday

5
Tuesday

6
Wednesday

7
Thursday

8
Friday

9
Saturday

Notes

10
Sunday

April

S	M	T	W	T	F	S
					1	2
3	4	5	6	7	8	9
10	11	12	13	14	15	16
17	18	19	20	21	22	23
24	25	26	27	28	29	30

Priorities

No. 1 ....

No. 2 ....

No. 3 ....

Goals

1. ....
2. ....
3. ....
4. ....
5. ....

Activities & Fitness

Mon ....

Tue ....

Wed ....

Thur ....

Fri ....

Sat ....

Sun ....

"Don't be busy. Be productive."

11
Monday

12
Tuesday

13
Wednesday

14
Thursday

15
Friday

16
Saturday

Notes

17
Sunday

April

S	M	T	W	T	F	S
					1	2
3	4	5	6	7	8	9
10	11	12	13	14	15	16
17	18	19	20	21	22	23
24	25	26	27	28	29	30

Priorities

No. 1

No. 2

No. 3

Goals

1.

2.

3.

4.

5.

Activities & Fitness

Mon

Tue

Wed

Thur

Fri

Sat

Sun

"No one is you and that is your power."

18
Monday

19
Tuesday

20
Wednesday

21
Thursday

22
Friday

23
Saturday

Notes

24
Sunday

April

S	M	T	W	T	F	S
					1	2
3	4	5	6	7	8	9
10	11	12	13	14	15	16
17	18	19	20	21	22	23
24	25	26	27	28	29	30

Priorities

No. 1 ....

No. 2 ....

No. 3 ....

Goals

1. ....
2. ....
3. ....
4. ....
5. ....

Activities & Fitness

Mon ....

Tue ....

Wed ....

Thur ....

Fri ....

Sat ....

Sun ....

"Take the risk or lose the chance."

25
Monday

26
Tuesday

27
Wednesday

28
Thursday

29
Friday

30
Saturday

*This week
I am grateful for*

Notes

1
Sunday

Habit Tracker

COLOR   ESSENTIAL HABITS

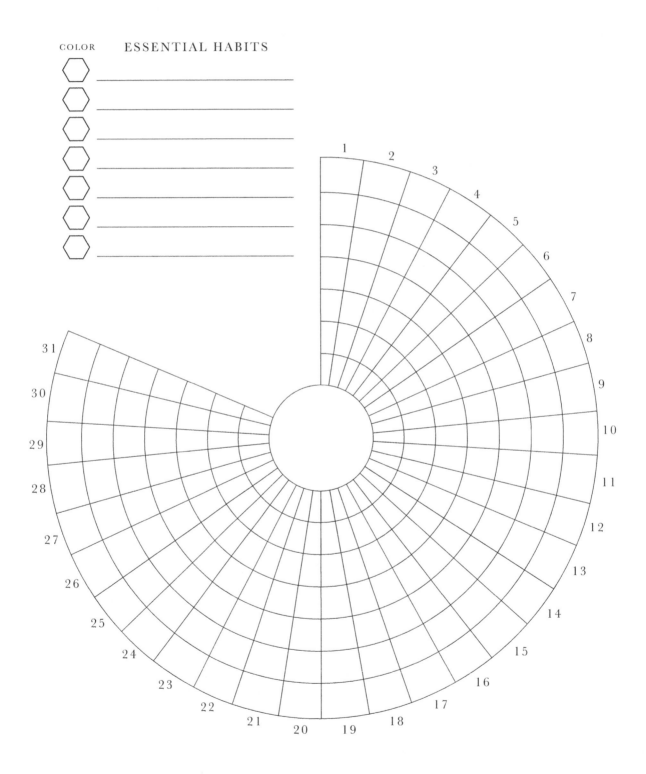

Mood Tracker

COLOR YOUR MOOD

HAPPY	SAD	TIRED	MOTIVATED	SICK
FOCUSED	STRESSED	EXCITED	ANGRY	ANXIOUS

05

Notes

May

Sunday	Monday	Tuesday
24	25	26
1	2	3
MOTHER'S DAY 8	9	10
15	16	17
22	23	24
29	MEMORIAL DAY 30	31

*"Do what you feel in your heart to be right -
for you'll be criticized anyway."*
- *ELEANOR ROOSEVELT*

2022

Wednesday	Thursday	Friday	Saturday
27	28	29	30
4	Cinco de Mayo 5	6	7
11	12	13	14
18	19	20	21
25	26	27	28
1	2	3	4

May

S	M	T	W	T	F	S
1	2	3	4	5	6	7
8	9	10	11	12	13	14
15	16	17	18	19	20	21
22	23	24	25	26	27	28

Priorities

No. 1 ....

No. 2 ....

No. 3 ....

Goals

1. ....

2. ....

3. ....

4. ....

5. ....

Activities & Fitness

Mon ....

Tue ....

Wed ....

Thur ....

Fri ....

Sat ....

Sun ....

"Once you become fearless, life becomes limitless."

2
Monday

3
Tuesday

4
Wednesday

5
Thursday

Notes

6
Friday

7
Saturday

8
Sunday

May

S	M	T	W	T	F	S
1	2	3	4	5	6	7
8	9	10	11	12	13	14
15	16	17	18	19	20	21
22	23	24	25	26	27	28

Priorities

No. 1
No. 2
No. 3

Goals

1.
2.
3.
4.
5.

Activities & Fitness

Mon
Tue
Wed
Thur
Fri
Sat
Sun

"Become the hardest working person you know."

9
Monday

10
Tuesday

11
Wednesday

12
Thursday

Notes

13
Friday

14
Saturday

15
Sunday

May

S	M	T	W	T	F	S
1	2	3	4	5	6	7
8	9	10	11	12	13	14
15	16	17	18	19	20	21
22	23	24	25	26	27	28

Priorities

No. 1 ....

No. 2 ....

No. 3 ....

Goals

1. ....

2. ....

3. ....

4. ....

5. ....

Activities & Fitness

Mon ....

Tue ....

Wed ....

Thur ....

Fri ....

Sat ....

Sun ....

"Don't give up,
don't take anything personally,
and don't take no for an answer."

16
Monday

17
Tuesday

18
Wednesday

19
Thursday

20
Friday

21
Saturday

Notes

22
Sunday

May

S	M	T	W	T	F	S
1	2	3	4	5	6	7
8	9	10	11	12	13	14
15	16	17	18	19	20	21
22	23	24	25	26	27	28

Priorities

No. 1 ....

No. 2 ....

No. 3 ....

Goals

1. ....
2. ....
3. ....
4. ....
5. ....

Activities & Fitness

Mon ....

Tue ....

Wed ....

Thur ....

Fri ....

Sat ....

Sun ....

"If you're terrified of what's next, you're on the right track."

23
Monday

24
Tuesday

25
Wednesday

26
Thursday

27
Friday

28
Saturday

29
Sunday

*This week
I am grateful for*

Notes

Habit Tracker

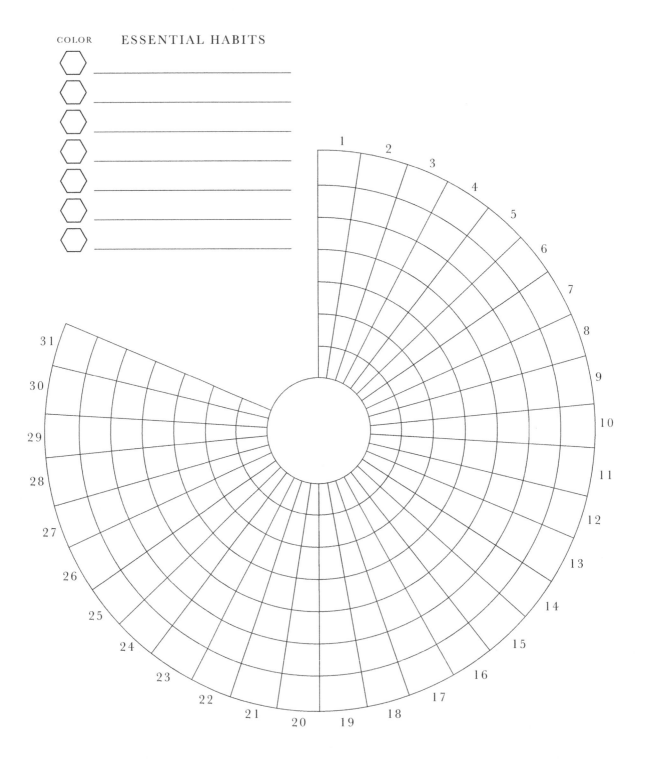

COLOR   ESSENTIAL HABITS

Mood Tracker

COLOR YOUR MOOD

HAPPY	SAD	TIRED	MOTIVATED	SICK
FOCUSED	STRESSED	EXCITED	ANGRY	ANXIOUS

1 8 2 7 17
12 6 25
24 14 4
23 20 31
30 10
29 5 19
21 27 15
18 11
3 26 13
16 9
28 22

06

Notes ....

June

Sunday	Monday	Tuesday
29	30	31
5	6	7
12	13	14
19 FATHER'S DAY	20	21 FIRST DAY OF SUMMER
26	27	28

"Step out of the history that is holding you back.
Step into the new story you are willing to create."
        - *OPRAH WINFREY*

2022

Wednesday	Thursday	Friday	Saturday
1	2	3	4
8	9	10	11
15	16	17	18
22	23	24	25
29	30	1	2

June

S	M	T	W	T	F	S
			1	2	3	4
5	6	7	8	9	10	11
12	13	14	15	16	17	18
19	20	21	22	23	24	25
26	27	28	29	30		

Priorities

No. 1

No. 2

No. 3

Goals

1.

2.

3.

4.

5.

Activities & Fitness

Mon

Tue

Wed

Thur

Fri

Sat

Sun

"It's always a good day to look good and make money."

30
Monday

31
Tuesday

1
Wednesday

2
Thursday

3
Friday

4
Saturday

Notes

5
Sunday

June

S	M	T	W	T	F	S
			1	2	3	4
5	6	7	8	9	10	11
12	13	14	15	16	17	18
19	20	21	22	23	24	25
26	27	28	29	30		

Priorities

No. 1 ....

No. 2 ....

No. 3 ....

Goals

1. ....
2. ....
3. ....
4. ....
5. ....

Activities & Fitness

Mon ....

Tue ....

Wed ....

Thur ....

Fri ....

Sat ....

Sun ....

"Slay your day."

6
Monday

7
Tuesday

8
Wednesday

9
Thursday

Notes

10
Friday

11
Saturday

12
Sunday

June

S	M	T	W	T	F	S
			1	2	3	4
5	6	7	8	9	10	11
12	13	14	15	16	17	18
19	20	21	22	23	24	25
26	27	28	29	30		

Priorities

No. 1 ....

No. 2 ....

No. 3 ....

Goals

1. ....
2. ....
3. ....
4. ....
5. ....

Activities & Fitness

Mon ....

Tue ....

Wed ....

Thur ....

Fri ....

Sat ....

Sun ....

"Boss up."

13
Monday

14
Tuesday

15
Wednesday

16
Thursday

17
Friday

18
Saturday

Notes

19
Sunday

June

S	M	T	W	T	F	S
			1	2	3	4
5	6	7	8	9	10	11
12	13	14	15	16	17	18
19	20	21	22	23	24	25
26	27	28	29	30		

Priorities

No. 1 ....

No. 2 ....

No. 3 ....

Goals

1. ....
2. ....
3. ....
4. ....
5. ....

Activities & Fitness

Mon ....

Tue ....

Wed ....

Thur ....

Fri ....

Sat ....

Sun ....

"Work hard in silence,
let success be your noise."

20
Monday

21
Tuesday

22
Wednesday

23
Thursday

Notes

24
Friday

25
Saturday

26
Sunday

Habit Tracker

COLOR   ESSENTIAL HABITS

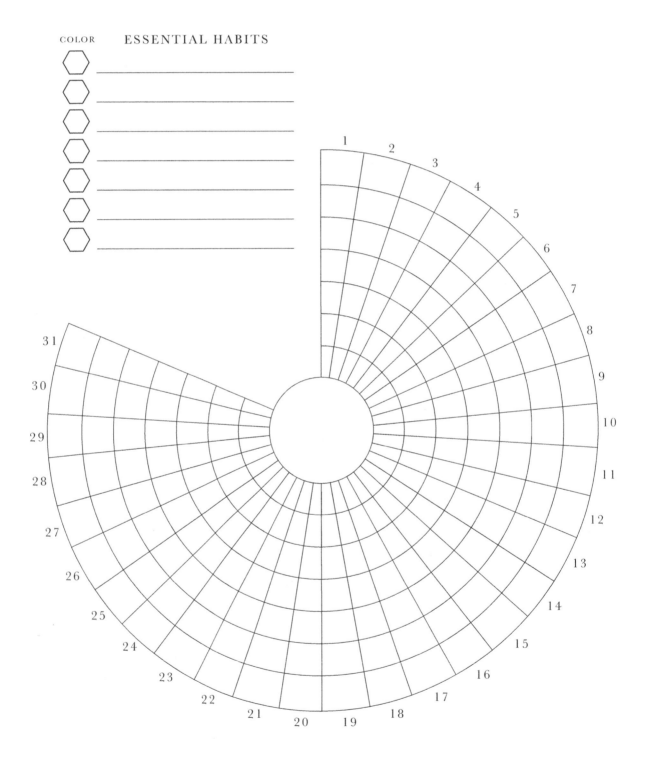

Mood Tracker

COLOR YOUR MOOD

HAPPY	SAD	TIRED	MOTIVATED	SICK

FOCUSED	STRESSED	EXCITED	ANGRY	ANXIOUS

07

July

Sunday	Monday	Tuesday
26	27	28
3	Independence Day 4	5
10	11	12
17	18	19
24	25	26
31	1	2

2022

Wednesday	Thursday	Friday	Saturday
29	30	1	2
6	7	8	9
13	14	15	16
20	21	22	23
27	28	29	30
3	4	5	6

July

S	M	T	W	T	F	S
					1	2
3	4	5	6	7	8	9
10	11	12	13	14	15	16
17	18	19	20	21	22	23
24	25	26	27	28	29	30
31						

Priorities

No. 1 ....

No. 2 ....

No. 3 ....

Goals

1. ....
2. ....
3. ....
4. ....
5. ....

Activities & Fitness

Mon ....

Tue ....

Wed ....

Thur ....

Fri ....

Sat ....

Sun ....

"Mood: unapologetically ambitious."

27
Monday

28
Tuesday

29
Wednesday

30
Thursday

1
Friday

2
Saturday

This week
I am grateful for

Notes

3
Sunday

July

S	M	T	W	T	F	S
					1	2
3	4	5	6	7	8	9
10	11	12	13	14	15	16
17	18	19	20	21	22	23
24	25	26	27	28	29	30
31						

Priorities

No. 1

No. 2

No. 3

Goals

1.

2.

3.

4.

5.

Activities & Fitness

Mon

Tue

Wed

Thur

Fri

Sat

Sun

*"I believe I can,
so I will."*

4
Monday

5
Tuesday

6
Wednesday

7
Thursday

Notes

8
Friday

9
Saturday

10
Sunday

July

S	M	T	W	T	F	S
					1	2
3	4	5	6	7	8	9
10	11	12	13	14	15	16
17	18	19	20	21	22	23
24	25	26	27	28	29	30
31						

Priorities

No. 1 ....

No. 2 ....

No. 3 ....

Goals

1. ....
2. ....
3. ....
4. ....
5. ....

Activities & Fitness

Mon ....

Tue ....

Wed ....

Thur ....

Fri ....

Sat ....

Sun ....

*"When things change inside you,
things change around you."*

11
Monday

12
Tuesday

13
Wednesday

14
Thursday

15
Friday

16
Saturday

Notes

17
Sunday

July

S	M	T	W	T	F	S
					1	2
3	4	5	6	7	8	9
10	11	12	13	14	15	16
17	18	19	20	21	22	23
24	25	26	27	28	29	30
31						

Priorities

No. 1

No. 2

No. 3

Goals

1.

2.

3.

4.

5.

Activities & Fitness

Mon

Tue

Wed

Thur

Fri

Sat

Sun

"Be you,
do you,
for you."

18
Monday

19
Tuesday

20
Wednesday

21
Thursday

22
Friday

23
Saturday

Notes

24
Sunday

July

S	M	T	W	T	F	S
					1	2
3	4	5	6	7	8	9
10	11	12	13	14	15	16
17	18	19	20	21	22	23
24	25	26	27	28	29	30
31						

Priorities

No. 1 ....

No. 2 ....

No. 3 ....

Goals

1. ....
2. ....
3. ....
4. ....
5. ....

Activities & Fitness

Mon ....

Tue ....

Wed ....

Thur ....

Fri ....

Sat ....

Sun ....

"Go girl, go!"

25
Monday

26
Tuesday

27
Wednesday

28
Thursday

29
Friday

30
Saturday

*This week
I am grateful for*

Notes

31
Sunday

Habit Tracker

COLOR   ESSENTIAL HABITS

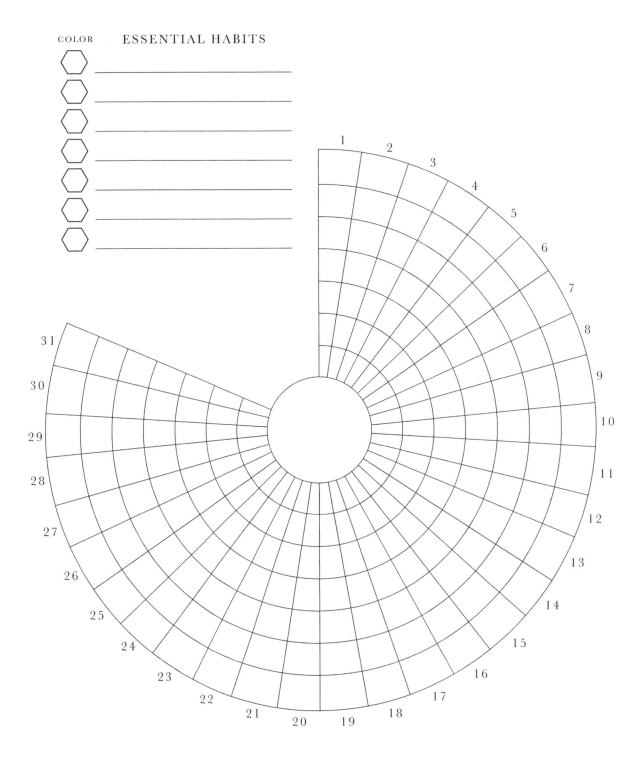

Mood Tracker

COLOR YOUR MOOD

HAPPY	SAD	TIRED	MOTIVATED	SICK
☐	☐	☐	☐	☐

FOCUSED	STRESSED	EXCITED	ANGRY	ANXIOUS
☐	☐	☐	☐	☐

1
8
2
7
17
12
6
25
24
14
4
23
20
31
30
10
29
5
19
21
27
15
18
11
3
26
13
16
9
28
22

08

August

Sunday	Monday	Tuesday
31	1	2
7	8	9
14	15	16
21	22	23
28	29	30

"Change your life today. Don't gamble on the future,
act now, without delay."
- *SIMONE DE BEAUVOIR*

2022

Wednesday	Thursday	Friday	Saturday
3	4	5	6
10	11	12	13
17	18	19	20
24	25	26	27
31	1	2	3

August

S	M	T	W	T	F	S
	1	2	3	4	5	6
7	8	9	10	11	12	13
14	15	16	17	18	19	20
21	22	23	24	25	26	27
28	29	30	31			

Priorities

No. 1

No. 2

No. 3

Goals

1.

2.

3.

4.

5.

Activities & Fitness

Mon

Tue

Wed

Thur

Fri

Sat

Sun

"Empowered women empower women."

1
Monday

2
Tuesday

3
Wednesday

4
Thursday

5
Friday

Notes

6
Saturday

7
Sunday

August

S	M	T	W	T	F	S
		1	2	3	4	5	6
7	8	9	10	11	12	13
14	15	16	17	18	19	20
21	22	23	24	25	26	27
28	29	30	31			

Priorities

No. 1
No. 2
No. 3

Goals

1.
2.
3.
4.
5.

Activities & Fitness

Mon
Tue
Wed
Thur
Fri
Sat
Sun

*"Don't underestimate the value
of investing in yourself."*

8
Monday

9
Tuesday

10
Wednesday

11
Thursday

12
Friday

13
Saturday

Notes

14
Sunday

August

S	M	T	W	T	F	S
		1	2	3	4	5	6
7	8	9	10	11	12	13
14	15	16	17	18	19	20
21	22	23	24	25	26	27
28	29	30	31			

Priorities

No. 1 ....

No. 2 ....

No. 3 ....

Goals

1. ....

2. ....

3. ....

4. ....

5. ....

Activities & Fitness

Mon ....

Tue ....

Wed ....

Thur ....

Fri ....

Sat ....

Sun ....

*"Be happy with what you have,
while working for what you want."*

15
Monday

16
Tuesday

17
Wednesday

18
Thursday

19
Friday

20
Saturday

Notes

21
Sunday

August

S	M	T	W	T	F	S
		1	2	3	4	5	6
7	8	9	10	11	12	13
14	15	16	17	18	19	20
21	22	23	24	25	26	27
28	29	30	31			

Priorities

No. 1 ....

No. 2 ....

No. 3 ....

Goals

1. ....

2. ....

3. ....

4. ....

5. ....

Activities & Fitness

Mon ....

Tue ....

Wed ....

Thur ....

Fri ....

Sat ....

Sun ....

"Kind heart, fierce mind, brave spirit."

22
Monday

23
Tuesday

24
Wednesday

25
Thursday

26
Friday

27
Saturday

*This week
I am grateful for*

Notes

28
Sunday

Habit Tracker

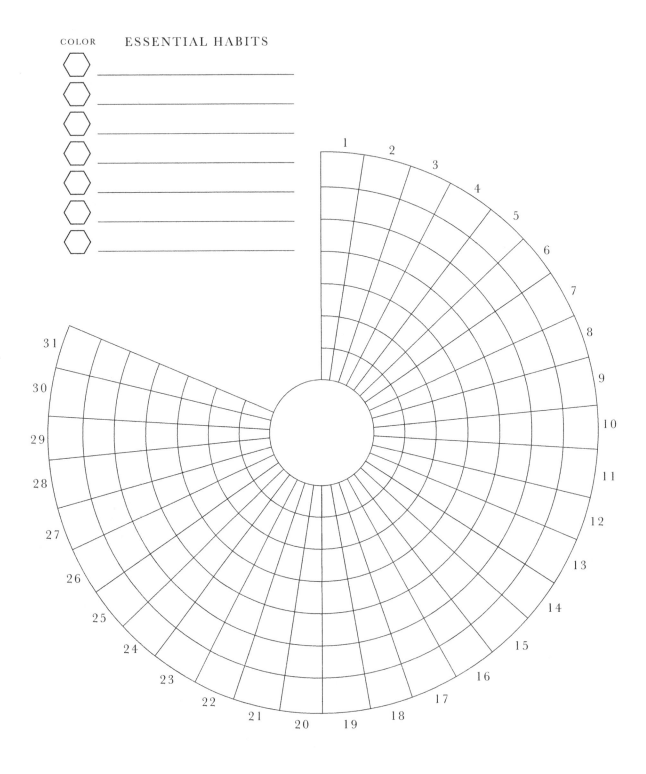

COLOR   ESSENTIAL HABITS

Mood Tracker

COLOR YOUR MOOD

HAPPY	SAD	TIRED	MOTIVATED	SICK

FOCUSED	STRESSED	EXCITED	ANGRY	ANXIOUS

09

September

Sunday	Monday	Tuesday
28	29	30
4	LABOR DAY 5	6
NATIONAL GRANDPARENTS DAY PATRIOT DAY 11	12	13
18	19	20
ROSH HASHANAH, BEGINS AT SUNSET 25	26	27

15
Thursday

16
Friday

17
Saturday

*This week
I am grateful for*

Notes

18
Sunday

September

S	M	T	W	T	F	S
				1	2	3
4	5	6	7	8	9	10
11	12	13	14	15	16	17
18	19	20	21	22	23	24
25	26	27	28	29	30	

Priorities

No. 1 ....

No. 2 ....

No. 3 ....

Goals

1. ....

2. ....

3. ....

4. ....

5. ....

Activities & Fitness

Mon ....

Tue ....

Wed ....

Thur ....

Fri ....

Sat ....

Sun ....

*"If you get tired, learn to rest
not to quit."*

19
Monday

20
Tuesday

21
Wednesday

22
Thursday

23
Friday

24
Saturday

Notes

25
Sunday

September

S	M	T	W	T	F	S
				1	2	3
4	5	6	7	8	9	10
11	12	13	14	15	16	17
18	19	20	21	22	23	24
25	26	27	28	29	30	

Priorities

No. 1 ....

No. 2 ....

No. 3 ....

Goals

1. ....
2. ....
3. ....
4. ....
5. ....

Activities & Fitness

Mon ....

Tue ....

Wed ....

Thur ....

Fri ....

Sat ....

Sun ....

*"Darling, chase goals
not people."*

26
Monday

27
Tuesday

28
Wednesday

29
Thursday

30
Friday

1
Saturday

*This week
I am grateful for*

Notes

2
Sunday

Habit Tracker

COLOR   ESSENTIAL HABITS

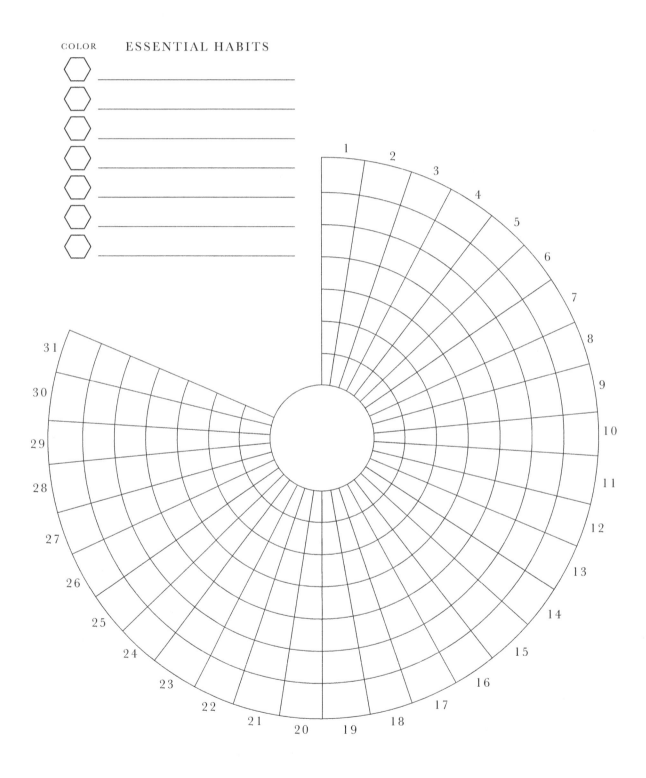

Mood Tracker

COLOR YOUR MOOD

HAPPY	SAD	TIRED	MOTIVATED	SICK
☐	☐	☐	☐	☐

FOCUSED	STRESSED	EXCITED	ANGRY	ANXIOUS
☐	☐	☐	☐	☐

10

October

Sunday	Monday	Tuesday
25	26	27
2	3	YOM KIPPUR, BEGINS AT SUNSET 4
9	COLUMBUS DAY 10	11
16	17	18
23	24	25
30	HALLOWEEN 31	1

September

S	M	T	W	T	F	S
				1	2	3
4	5	6	7	8	9	10
11	12	13	14	15	16	17
18	19	20	21	22	23	24
25	26	27	28	29	30	

Priorities

No. 1 ....

No. 2 ....

No. 3 ....

Goals

1. ....
2. ....
3. ....
4. ....
5. ....

Activities & Fitness

Mon ....

Tue ....

Wed ....

Thur ....

Fri ....

Sat ....

Sun ....

"'Stress does not go with my outfit."

5
Monday

6
Tuesday

7
Wednesday

1
Thursday

2
Friday

3
Saturday

This week
I am grateful for

Notes

4
Sunday

September

S	M	T	W	T	F	S
				1	2	3
4	5	6	7	8	9	10
11	12	13	14	15	16	17
18	19	20	21	22	23	24
25	26	27	28	29	30	

Priorities

No. 1

No. 2

No. 3

Goals

1.

2.

3.

4.

5.

Activities & Fitness

Mon

Tue

Wed

Thur

Fri

Sat

Sun

"BRB, manifesting the life of my dreams."

12
Monday

13
Tuesday

14
Wednesday

8
Thursday

*This week
I am grateful for*

Notes

9
Friday

10
Saturday

11
Sunday

2022

Wednesday	Thursday	Friday	Saturday
31	1	2	3
7	8	9	10
14	15	16	17
21	22 FIRST DAY OF AUTUMN	23	24
28	29	30	1

September

S	M	T	W	T	F	S
				1	2	3
4	5	6	7	8	9	10
11	12	13	14	15	16	17
18	19	20	21	22	23	24
25	26	27	28	29	30	

Priorities

No. 1
No. 2
No. 3

Goals

1.
2.
3.
4.
5.

Activities & Fitness

Mon
Tue
Wed
Thur
Fri
Sat
Sun

*"Coffee in one hand,
confidence in the other."*

29
Monday

30
Tuesday

31
Wednesday

"Normal is not something to aspire to,
it's something to get away from."
- JODIE FOSTER

2022

Wednesday	Thursday	Friday	Saturday
28	29	30	1
5	6	7	8
12	13	14	15
19	20	21	22
26	27	28	29
2	3	4	5

October

S	M	T	W	T	F	S
						1
2	3	4	5	6	7	8
9	10	11	12	13	14	15
16	17	18	19	20	21	22
23	24	25	26	27	28	29
30	31					

Priorities

No. 1 ....

No. 2 ....

No. 3 ....

Goals

1. ....
2. ....
3. ....
4. ....
5. ....

Activities & Fitness

Mon ....

Tue ....

Wed ....

Thur ....

Fri ....

Sat ....

Sun ....

"Starve your distractions,
feed your focus."

3
Monday

4
Tuesday

5
Wednesday

6
Thursday

7
Friday

8
Saturday

*This week
I am grateful for*

Notes

9
Sunday

October

S	M	T	W	T	F	S
						1
2	3	4	5	6	7	8
9	10	11	12	13	14	15
16	17	18	19	20	21	22
23	24	25	26	27	28	29
30	31					

Priorities

No. 1 ....

No. 2 ....

No. 3 ....

Goals

1. ....
2. ....
3. ....
4. ....
5. ....

Activities & Fitness

Mon ....

Tue ....

Wed ....

Thur ....

Fri ....

Sat ....

Sun ....

*"You are what you do,
not what you say you will do."*

10
Monday

11
Tuesday

12
Wednesday

13
Thursday

14
Friday

15
Saturday

Notes

16
Sunday

October

S	M	T	W	T	F	S
						1
2	3	4	5	6	7	8
9	10	11	12	13	14	15
16	17	18	19	20	21	22
23	24	25	26	27	28	29
30	31					

Priorities

No. 1

No. 2

No. 3

Goals

1.

2.

3.

4.

5.

Activities & Fitness

Mon

Tue

Wed

Thur

Fri

Sat

Sun

"Be the kind of person that makes other people want to up their game."

17
Monday

18
Tuesday

19
Wednesday

20
Thursday

Notes

21
Friday

22
Saturday

23
Sunday

October

S	M	T	W	T	F	S
						1
2	3	4	5	6	7	8
9	10	11	12	13	14	15
16	17	18	19	20	21	22
23	24	25	26	27	28	29
30	31					

Priorities

No. 1

No. 2

No. 3

Goals

1.
2.
3.
4.
5.

Activities & Fitness

Mon
Tue
Wed
Thur
Fri
Sat
Sun

"Results happen over time, not overnight."

24
Monday

25
Tuesday

26
Wednesday

27
Thursday

28
Friday

29
Saturday

Notes

30
Sunday

Habit Tracker

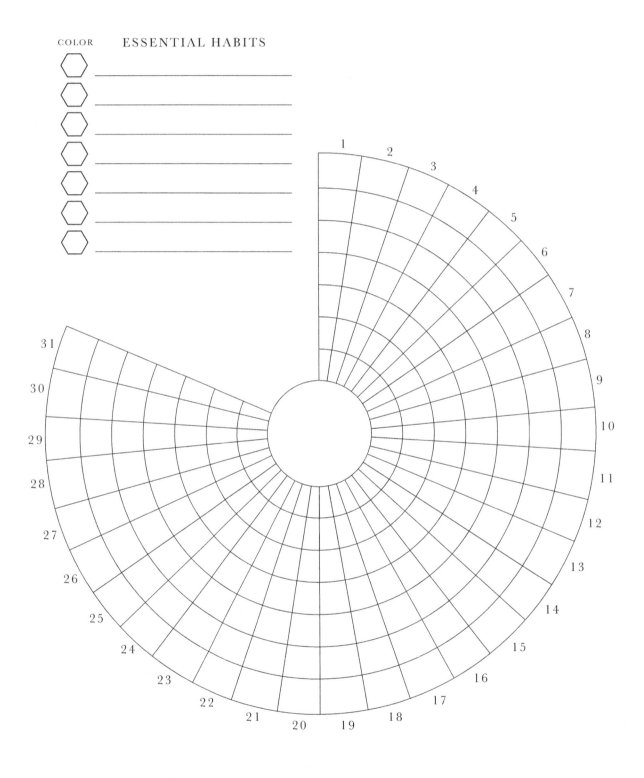

COLOR   ESSENTIAL HABITS

Mood Tracker

COLOR YOUR MOOD

HAPPY	SAD	TIRED	MOTIVATED	SICK

FOCUSED	STRESSED	EXCITED	ANGRY	ANXIOUS

11

November

Sunday	Monday	Tuesday
30	31	1
DAYLIGHT SAVING TIME ENDS 6	7	ELECTION DAY 8
13	14	15
20	21	22
27	CYBER MONDAY 28	29

"If you're offered a seat on a rocket ship,
don't ask what seat! Just get on."
- SHERYL SANDBERG

2022

Wednesday	Thursday	Friday	Saturday
2	3	4	5
9	10	VETERANS DAY 11	12
16	17	18	19
23	THANKSGIVING DAY 24	BLACK FRIDAY 25	26
30	1	2	3

November

S	M	T	W	T	F	S
		1	2	3	4	5
6	7	8	9	10	11	12
13	14	15	16	17	18	19
20	21	22	23	24	25	26
27	28	20	30			

Priorities

No. 1 ....

No. 2 ....

No. 3 ....

Goals

1. ....
2. ....
3. ....
4. ....
5. ....

Activities & Fitness

Mon ....

Tue ....

Wed ....

Thur ....

Fri ....

Sat ....

Sun ....

"Girl, you already have what it takes."

31
Monday

1
Tuesday

2
Wednesday

3
Thursday

....
....
....
....
....

4
Friday

....
....
....
....
....

5
Saturday

....
....
....
....
....

This week I am grateful for

....
....
....

Notes

....
....
....
....
....
....
....
....

6
Sunday

....
....
....
....
....

November

S	M	T	W	T	F	S
		1	2	3	4	5
6	7	8	9	10	11	12
13	14	15	16	17	18	19
20	21	22	23	24	25	26
27	28	20	30			

Priorities

No. 1 ....

No. 2 ....

No. 3 ....

Goals

1. ....
2. ....
3. ....
4. ....
5. ....

Activities & Fitness

Mon ....

Tue ....

Wed ....

Thur ....

Fri ....

Sat ....

Sun ....

"Each day you must choose: the pain of discipline or the pain of regret."

7
Monday

8
Tuesday

9
Wednesday

10
Thursday

11
Friday

12
Saturday

Notes

13
Sunday

November

S	M	T	W	T	F	S
		1	2	3	4	5
6	7	8	9	10	11	12
13	14	15	16	17	18	19
20	21	22	23	24	25	26
27	28	20	30			

Priorities

No. 1 ....

No. 2 ....

No. 3 ....

Goals

1. ....

2. ....

3. ....

4. ....

5. ....

Activities & Fitness

Mon ....

Tue ....

Wed ....

Thur ....

Fri ....

Sat ....

Sun ....

*"If the plan doesn't work,
change the plan - not the goal."*

14
Monday

15
Tuesday

16
Wednesday

17
Thursday

18
Friday

19
Saturday

20
Sunday

This week I am grateful for

Notes

November

S	M	T	W	T	F	S
		1	2	3	4	5
6	7	8	9	10	11	12
13	14	15	16	17	18	19
20	21	22	23	24	25	26
27	28	20	30			

Priorities

No. 1 ....

No. 2 ....

No. 3 ....

Goals

1. ....

2. ....

3. ....

4. ....

5. ....

Activities & Fitness

Mon ....

Tue ....

Wed ....

Thur ....

Fri ....

Sat ....

Sun ....

"Be so good they can't ignore you."

21
Monday

22
Tuesday

23
Wednesday

24
Thursday

25
Friday

26
Saturday

*This week
I am grateful for*

Notes

27
Sunday

Habit Tracker

COLOR   ESSENTIAL HABITS

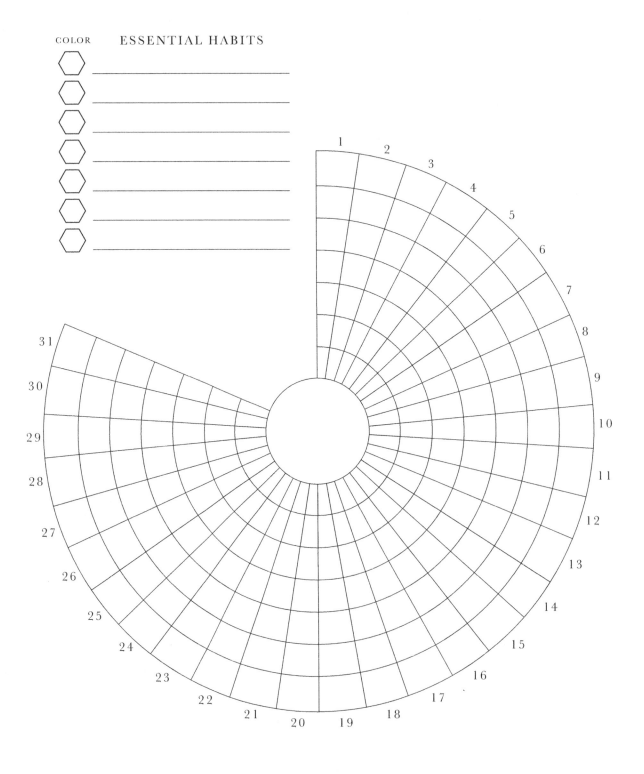

Mood Tracker

COLOR YOUR MOOD

HAPPY	SAD	TIRED	MOTIVATED	SICK

FOCUSED	STRESSED	EXCITED	ANGRY	ANXIOUS

12

December

Sunday	Monday	Tuesday
27	28	29
4	5	6
11	12	13
Hanukkah, Begins at Sunset 18	19	20
Christmas Day 25	26	27

2022

Wednesday	Thursday	Friday	Saturday
30	1	2	3
7	8	9	10
14	15	16	17
FIRST DAY OF WINTER 21	22	23	CHRISTMAS EVE 24
28	29	30	NEW YEAR'S EVE 31

December

S	M	T	W	T	F	S
				1	2	3
4	5	6	7	8	9	10
11	12	13	14	15	16	17
18	19	20	21	22	23	24
25	26	27	28	29	30	31

Priorities

No. 1 ....

No. 2 ....

No. 3 ....

Goals

1. ....

2. ....

3. ....

4. ....

5. ....

Activities & Fitness

Mon ....

Tue ....

Wed ....

Thur ....

Fri ....

Sat ....

Sun ....

"A river cuts through rock, not because of power but because of persistence."

28
Monday

29
Tuesday

30
Wednesday

1
Thursday

2
Friday

3
Saturday

This week I am grateful for

Notes

4
Sunday

December

S	M	T	W	T	F	S
				1	2	3
4	5	6	7	8	9	10
11	12	13	14	15	16	17
18	19	20	21	22	23	24
25	26	27	28	29	30	31

Priorities

No. 1 ....
No. 2 ....
No. 3 ....

Goals

1. ....
2. ....
3. ....
4. ....
5. ....

Activities & Fitness

Mon ....
Tue ....
Wed ....
Thur ....
Fri ....
Sat ....
Sun ....

*"Wake up beauty,
it's time to beast!"*

5
Monday

6
Tuesday

7
Wednesday

8
Thursday

Notes

9
Friday

10
Saturday

11
Sunday

December

S	M	T	W	T	F	S
				1	2	3
4	5	6	7	8	9	10
11	12	13	14	15	16	17
18	19	20	21	22	23	24
25	26	27	28	29	30	31

Priorities

No. 1 ....

No. 2 ....

No. 3 ....

Goals

1. ....
2. ....
3. ....
4. ....
5. ....

Activities & Fitness

Mon ....

Tue ....

Wed ....

Thur ....

Fri ....

Sat ....

Sun ....

*"Don't give up what you want most,
for what you want now."*

12
Monday

13
Tuesday

14
Wednesday

15
Thursday

16
Friday

17
Saturday

*This week
I am grateful for*

Notes

18
Sunday

December

S	M	T	W	T	F	S
				1	2	3
4	5	6	7	8	9	10
11	12	13	14	15	16	17
18	19	20	21	22	23	24
25	26	27	28	29	30	31

Priorities

No. 1 ....

No. 2 ....

No. 3 ....

Goals

1. ....

2. ....

3. ....

4. ....

5. ....

Activities & Fitness

Mon ....

Tue ....

Wed ....

Thur ....

Fri ....

Sat ....

Sun ....

*"I'm coming for everything
they said I couldn't have."*

19
Monday

20
Tuesday

21
Wednesday

22
Thursday

23
Friday

24
Saturday

*This week
I am grateful for*

Notes

25
Sunday

December

S	M	T	W	T	F	S
				1	2	3
4	5	6	7	8	9	10
11	12	13	14	15	16	17
18	19	20	21	22	23	24
25	26	27	28	29	30	31

Priorities

No. 1

No. 2

No. 3

Goals

1.

2.

3.

4.

5.

Activities & Fitness

Mon

Tue

Wed

Thur

Fri

Sat

Sun

"Never forget why you started."

26
Monday

27
Tuesday

28
Wednesday

29
Thursday

30
Friday

31
Saturday

Notes

1
Sunday

Habit Tracker

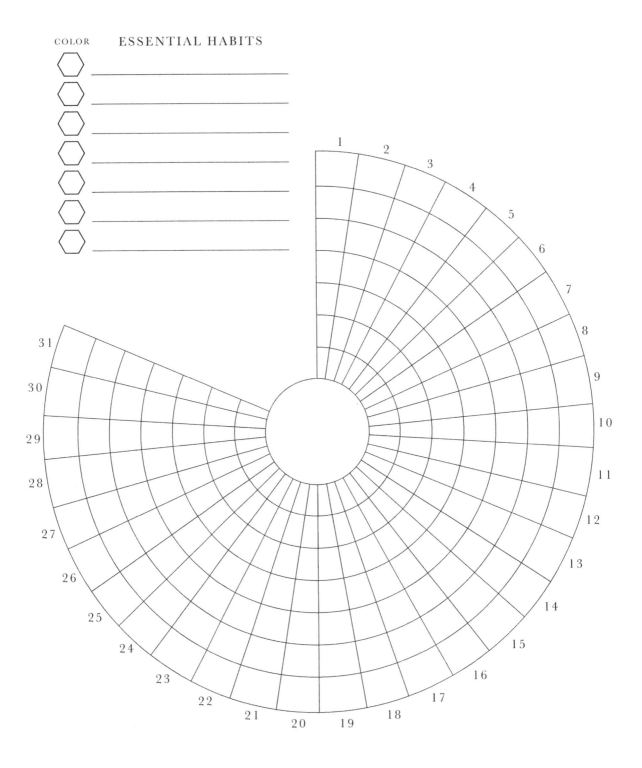

COLOR   ESSENTIAL HABITS

Mood Tracker

COLOR YOUR MOOD

HAPPY	SAD	TIRED	MOTIVATED	SICK
FOCUSED	STRESSED	EXCITED	ANGRY	ANXIOUS

Notes

Made in the USA
Coppell, TX
13 January 2022

71479342R00092